WHEN WORDS FLOW

*A cluster of poems and notes from
a woman and seeker of life*

Felecia Kearse

Copyright © 2021 by Felecia Kearse

All rights reserved.

The Awakened Press
www.theawakenedpress.com

The Awakened Press

Artwork by Felecia Kearse

Cover Design by David Moratto

Interior Design by Fabricio P. 7

No part of this publication may be reproduced, stored in a retrieval system, or transmitted in any form or by any means, electronic, mechanical, recording, or otherwise, without the prior written permission of the authors, except by a reviewer who wishes to quote brief passages in connection with a review written for inclusion in a print or online magazine, newspaper, periodical, blog, or broadcast.

First edition.

ISBN 978-1-989134-12-2

Amorita,

We get tangled often. Perplexed by every emotional string with taunt ties of there own. It can make our hearts tensed and our minds strangled to any clear sight. But, perhaps this part of your journey is one led by the unknown, as a deep and alluring hole to have these tangled strings release you into it — into a pit of re-creating yourself. May you enjoy the process of further creating this masterpiece that is you!

Contents

Genesis 2

Waking Up 12

Opening 34

Guided 50

Enduring 90

Growing 162

Let Life Be Bright 190

In Loving Memory 192

With Gratitude 194

Genesis

You may have many questions. You may be curiously seeking for the very meanings of your past and how they led you to this moment.

There is a beginning, a now, and the ongoing. Life moves like that of the wind hitting against you, like the water rippling or waving, like blood that swirls in your veins—all flowing and cycling.

Sometimes we find ourselves adrift and sinking, unable to scope our yearnings, sliding through the depths of depression, stalling the motion, being weighed by life deeper and deeper and hungry for discovery. But it takes a tiny seed of surrender to reveal the beautiful sounds and images of life, unfolding us out of those icky layers to a new platform to stand onto.

My friend, there is beauty held within the journey of becoming adrift; in being lost as we search for pieces that will mould to the very answers we are desperate to grasp. Know firmly that you will be unchained from it and you will make many discoveries, as I did. Through a wee number of years, I went from a curious but drifting being scavenging for the pieces—into a liberated woman of many findings, and many others yet to come.

These notes and poems I've written express my personal transformational experience through the years of 2016-2020 during my yoga journey. They hold a cluster of insights and lessons I'd scribbled in a journal to return to time and time again as leverage for what's to come on the horizon. They embody moments of the dark, the dazzling, of fear, love, the inspiring, of adventures within and out, and that of transformation. I share them with you to grab hold of them too, and use them as a tool into your own realm of self-realizations, awareness and transformations.

May you trust the journey. Trust in the way you move through it.

I believe that the moment I surrendered and opened myself, these revelations of poems and notes were flowing through me from the Divine/the God/the Universe/whatever you identify it as—flowing like a river that I just so happened to be present in. And my desire to express it made me the welcoming gate of receiving. They allowed me to fuel my motivation and mindset to the path that spread in front of me, to scope out how the past and its steps have truly defined my meaning.

Wherever you are in your life, may it be in the moments of dismay, rage, sorrow, warmth along cheeriness, of wonder, and peaks of wakefulness—all come into activity for the greater of purposes, as long as we allow ourselves to see it in the lens of purpose.

These words are planted before you to bring a helping hand to brighten your day; to propel you to see the beauty of your life and all its aspects and features into a collection of insights and lessons. This is where it can lift you to a true lesson through your own experience—something you have to find within yourself. Rather than dwelling in your murkiness it may ignite you from it and into the essence of light and love.

This is about learning to trust yourself in whatever process you are going through. Trust is like the movement of a flow: as flow can only happen when we trust it, in whatever flow that is and whatever form it comes in. This is about the flow within your personal experience and to truly stand within it. As you dig into the surfaces below each layer, you will identify the why within your own path from a conscious perspective and into a treasurable place.

You will explore the feeling as if plates are shifting, erupting awareness here and there, rising through the cracks and offering a grander view of where you stand. As I had welcomed the flow of these lessons through me like that of a river I found myself standing in, I share to you the beautiful meanings of it all when you welcome the flow to come passing through to you too.

I hope that wherever you are, this becomes an offering for you to feel comforted, supported, inspired, and motivated. To perhaps guide your own revelations and growth. To allow you to believe in your transformations and not be fearful as to where your heart feels ignited to go, to feel the beautiful meaning of life unearthing before your eyes, and hoping you energize to those visions in your own very heart.

So this collection of some of my unplanned writings, is a collection for you. Bringing forth the reminder to reflect on the lessons and growth we go through. To offer degrees of healing and to express them in whatever form you feel to share them in.

Just trust.

Felicia Pearse

Life,
Thank you for the events and beings that inspired
my revelations and feelings.

For you,
Wherever you may be.

Waking up

The truth about reality
Is that there is more to the initial view.
There are dimensions and layers
That have been shunned away from view.

As the snow shelters the withered
And freezes the present state,
We scope through the landscape
Into a white abyss.

Curious and inquired
By all things wee and big,
We are drawn by the snowflakes
That take us on a wild escape.

Diverse in patterns, timing, and size.
It all flowed from the same cloud in the vast sky.
There is a connection between you and I,
We are all one with a journey in mind.

Distinct in appearances, wants, and likes
With different ventures arranged by unseen existences.

This is awareness.
This is gratefulness.
This is revolutionary.
This is leading your own fate.

For every river
There flows new water.
Tick tick tock
The clock strikes a new number.

Tranquility is the best policy
When it steers to change.
Let the portal between your lungs
Be welcomed to any pathway you happen to trek on,
Both struggled and great.
Be aware that every moment is an expression
And a repetitive birth of a newer you.
So trust, and let the change shape you.

Allow your creativity
To stream out
And bask in its beauty,
For you'll notice
The nourishments
That it feeds you.

Grasp harder on life
The one you should truly live.
For excessive stress, work, and politics
Happens to not matter
When you're near the end.

Find those to love
And in return they love you back.
Find passion in something new
Or fall back in love with the fun stuff you used to do.
Find adventure that excites your veins
While checking off that bucket list.
Find strength to surpass your fears
And sometimes take a chance.
Remember the past
And collect more memories as you can.

Remember,
Tomorrow can always be our last.

Delve into the things
That your heart aches for,
Even when your thoughts
Over-float.

As the white abyss re-appears
We are reflected on the many layers
That we shed off
In previous years.

While this may steer us to old habits
Or plant us in the soil of puzzlement and irritation.
We are shepherded towards the light
That shines on us.

For without the awareness of the layers,
How could we alter through the chrysalis?
Through the gratefulness
Of where we've sprouted from,
We purge
Making leeway more vast
In our impending journey.

So, don't fear
It's all a transition from here.

Every steer we take
Is diverse from the last current we sailed.
We are only aware
Of what damaged us
Or what soothed us

As a catalyst to where we anchor now.

But from this station
To the next shore
We can't harness on preparation
For the sea will surprise and transform us even more.

The relieving feeling
When you grasp hold and haul out the deep roots
That lingered in the garden bed overtime.
To make leeway more vast
For new and impending life.

Balancing can be a juggling act at times,
If not all times.

As this appears
We veer in directions that stumble us in puzzlement
And in tempered manners.

Allow the notion of encountered unexpectedness
To sink into your awareness
With a full open heart.

For a full scripted pathway
Processed by you
Is detouring you
From the route made for you
But not by you.

Live from the heart
Allow your internal compass to steer you
As you handle the wheel with gentle grip
Merging the powers of you with the divine flow
Releasing resistance
And easing tension.

Never feel liable
To achieve a sum of desires
In one duration of time.

Disperse them
And give the time to accompany
Each of your aspirations
In leeway.

That leash gripping onto you
From a barricade wall force
May seem to detain you
From any release and freedom.

Countless times
You try to run forward
But then you slingback
Hitting a wall of bricks
Continuing to exist
Defeated by the weight of the past emotions, reckonings, and notions.

Lack of interest for departure
Then rules your being.
Overtaken,
You are blanketed
With numb and irked mannerisms.

Questions roam your mind,
How do you smash something so sturdy?
A vicious attack won't even scratch it.

As you ponder,
You set your eyes on the wall.
Brick by brick
You acknowledge
Its texture, colour, and level of layers.

At that moment of recognizing
The surface you felt,
The shade you saw,
And the phase you encountered,
You begin to admire it.

A colossal force
Comes across
Unlatching the leash from you.

You stare upon
That divine giant with gratitude
And dash away forward
Never fearsome of the barricade wall.

For you notice
That it's only an illusion
And a lesson
After all.

I'll forever
Rediscover
The map
Of myself.

In order for life
To blossom in the light,
The darkness shall be
The nourishing of the sprouting.

For without
The dampened and dark soil.
The roots,
Visible in the light,
Will wither
Hindering any life from growing.

Good old sky
Giving us the darkness,
The brightness
And brightness.

Aged in many moons
Swallowed by the limitless.
When crescent
Makes the critters
Cry for their awareness.
When full
Makes us
Shout for excitement.

Trees blanket
The moist ashes,
Upon the streams
That nourishes
Into the depths of our core,
We are lightness.

We stare down
Towards our roots,
Plunged into mother earth's floor
—Balanced.

Branches creep
As we stroll through the webs
That gate
The imprinted words that form a story
From one mother tree
To the next.

Beauty is endless
Existing in eternal shields
That cannot be combusted.

So, I will stare at it all
Feel the vibrational roars
That roam through my veins
Like echoes bouncing
In the concrete valleys
Of the caves.

I will indulge
In its beauty
Lend my ears
To the vibrant beat
Of my heart
And yours.

Let them beat
As one,
Let her sway
Through the scales
We play.

As we honour
The godly sounds,
The gods will honour
Our songs.

And you feel the vibes,
The vibes
In the valley.

Patterns reoccur
Such as patterns of self-loathing.
It trails along our path
In higher dosage
Than self-adoring.

We spend more feelings and thoughts
Unscrambling the puzzle pieces
Of us.
Assuring us
Bit by bit
As to why we aren't poised enough.

Mute the rotten memories
That created this fear.
Dismay,
As you'll learn,
Is not even real.

You are the author
of the book of you.
It'll take some time
But practice
Will fuel you.
As you charge,
You'll uncover
A solution.
Just two things
That will make life worth living.

Having trust and love,
Will be the medicine
For it all.

Opening

You only lose the things
That are no longer in need.
But you hold onto the ones
That keep you onto your feet.

For the horizon you scope,
Firmly peeling your peepers towards
And drawn by such anticipation,
Can easily be hidden
By such thick fog
Blindly navigating your course
To another outlook.

Don't fret,
Don't disregard.
There is a lesson to be altered
And a jolly reason
For such an alter.

Love all the lessons.

You are always
Steering towards the outcome
Of utmost happiness.

Trust it.

Go amongst
The unexplored horizons.
It may unfold
A new map
You unpredictably desire.

As the white abyss dissolves
Into the transition of rebirth,
Why do I mourn for the snow to preserve?
For I feel the desire
For such a sprouting,
Yet I have taken such an enjoyment
For the tranquil inward journey.

Perhaps for the reason
That the white landscapes
Offered me the directions
On how to peel off the non-core layers
That were latched onto me.
And in the process,
It showcased a fresher mould of me.

Perhaps, I blindly feel
There is a wee more to detach
In order to be enchanted
By my being.

Only the moment will reveal,
And the reveal will occur
In the unexpected moments.

But this winter
Has been a reward
And I am grateful.

Allow your deepest
And most tangled of roots
To absorb the nourishments.

Giving you the ability
To fully blossom
Towards the sun.

And so, the trails
You've begun to trek
Prevail ahead
Through the magical features that surround.

The markings are still seen,
The obvious sight
That they lead through
And on an ongoing journey,
The knowing
That you will pass through,
And the gratitude
That must be revealed
When you pace your speed
On the path
That's been created for you.

Find the adventure
Within the journey.
Patience.

A stroll in the woods
Becomes medicine
As the deep green
That surrounds you,
Holds the mightiest
Of all vibrations:
Love.

Do you ever stand still,
To witness
How the wind caresses the water
Ever so gently to its surface?

How a mere touch
Welcomes the intimacy
Between both elements
As it arouses degrees of motion?

Intimacy
In all forms
Is supremely persuasive.
Rather it be a contact
Between two individuals
Or thoughts merely provoking our feelings.

In the same way
The interconnection
Of any measure in our lives
Pushes motions
Onto our own surface.

Be mindful
Of what you welcome
And how it shifts you.

Love
Is the reminder
Of divine
That holds you.

Rooted to the soil of the Earth,
Stationed to the surface,
Reaching up to the mystery
Of the heavens.

Branches of all forms and lengths
Bonded to the vessel of the tree.
Weaving and parting amongst each other
And even towards the surrounding trees.

The crowns of the bodies
Sway and glide
Through the winds,
Like blood vessels pumping
Or electrifying neurons actively moving
Inside mankind.

The world around
Reflects the inner world
Of you and I.
Alive and revitalized.

Happiness
Is mostly achieved
By living
Presently.

There is something
Sensually marvelous
When we touch
Our own vessel
In a loving and caring way.

Rid the loath
Welcome the love
Feel the sensations
Of simply resting your hands
Upon your skin.

You then begin to appreciate
Your self.

Chaos in the mind
Creates a blinded view.
As you pace yourself,
Clarity is revealed,
Leaving you with a
Perceptive view.

Not even a farmer
Can maintain produce
For others,
When he himself,
Doesn't have the energy
To maintain it.

GUIDED

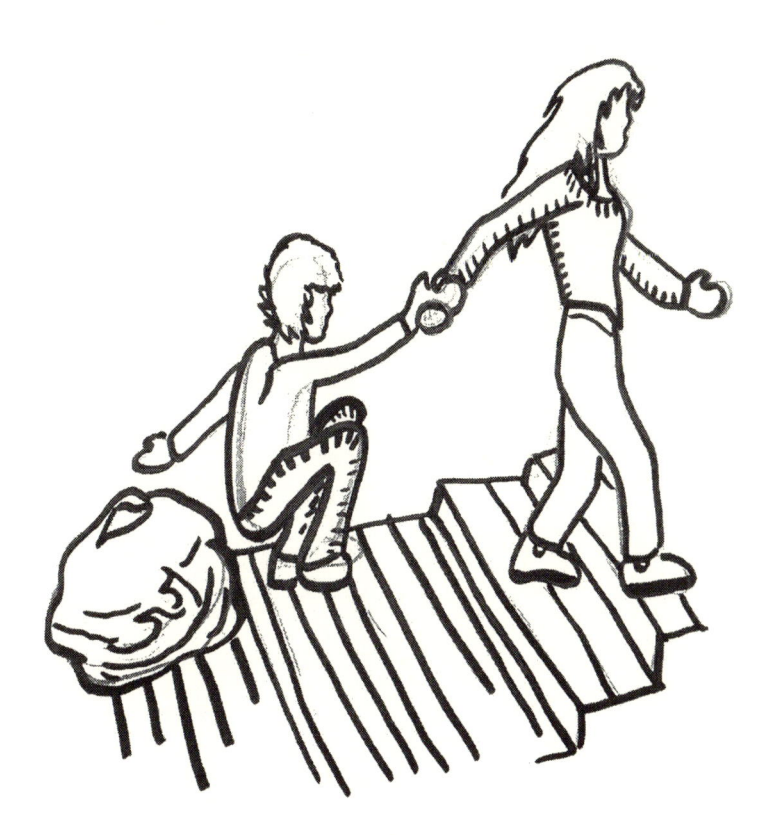

Sometimes
We follow
In a direction
That the surroundings
Takes us.

Dandelion

There are feelings emerging
Like dandelion seeds blowing.
I find myself twirling
To force them into dispersing.

For reasons to ignore
A giant patch of blossoms from appearing.
A potency of such feelings
Leave me in fear
For the sake of healing.
In fear for the lack of roaming.
In fear of no growing.

So here I spin my body
Palms waving the seeds around me
Blowing to all distances
Of the meadow
As the patches grow sporadically.

For this doesn't stick the feelings
Out of the land so obviously,
Rather blends into the spaces
In secrecy.

Revealing
Your emotions
Makes space
To reveal
Your strength.

Go for wherever
Your soul
Steers you.
Let no alternative
Influences
Control you.

Lead by
The freedom
Of love.
Don't let attachments
Crumble
Your potential
To grow.

Wherever you are,
Be reminded
That you carry those dearly
Within you
On your unforgettable journey.
Move on.

Brush off the self-attacks
And embrace the innocence of you
That you blindly see as a dunce.

Give tenderness
To your innocence
And you'll soon
Give tenderness
To the innocence
Of others.

Seek the humour
Of such mistakes and shame
That you allow
To bruise you.
Within time,
You'll uncover the lessons
That tried to capture you.

Your wounds may still be preserved
As you dissect blame
Towards you.

As you place yourself
In the pit of self-loath,
A thick guard appears
To prevent the similar actions
From drowning you.

The small pit confines you,
But you fear
The barriers
From exposing you.

Be reminded
That life nurtures you,
Protecting you always,
And gifting you
With the lessons
To shape you.

Calm your fearful barriers,
Slowly embrace yourself
And embrace the love
That surrounds you.

Loving every detail and being
In your days
That warm you.

And know that
You will receive
Waves of love
Back to you.

You are always loved.

Joy
Won't fade
You.

Joy
Will lift
You.

For every
Tear shed
Fills
A new
Purpose.

I've taken strides
I've taken tumbles
I've seen life through
Another tunnel.

"Be with me,"
She says at the mirror.

When you release
Your body and mind
From the sucking weight of aches,

You make space
Within for new and purposeful
Fillings.

Life keeps on propelling
And so should you.

Questions.
One upon the other,
Subjected to thoughts
Like wild currents of wind
In the vessel that I am in.

Such thickness
Makes it difficult
For my lungs to capture and release.
Something so vital
Has become too solid for me to breathe.

To be here in the moment
And be a part of a dream.

Sometimes
The path is smooth
And other times rough.
But the landscape
Is always there
To scope.

When you can't figure out your feelings,
Simply allow yourself
To feel your feelings.

There's a war
In our thoughts,
Leaving us sinking
In the mud.
Unforgiving and stuck.

Roots deep and scattered.
Wilted and shattered.
Tipping in the matter.
Not able to balance.

Yet the sun still shines.
Trying to capture our minds.
Unconditional in its offer.
Somehow, we still blind ourselves
From the light and offer.

It's a stable in our lives,
To rise our souls to fright.
That the darkness is nothing
But a feature on the side.

As you forgive,
You allow for nourishments.
To strengthen the roots below
And allow peace
To be in our thoughts.

You are always given enough fuel
To surpass the next kilometre in your journey.

Love always
Remains within.

Seek a home
In every place
And learn
A new aspect of yourself
To love
By those that are in every home.

Loneliness
Is the feeling
Of pain.
Where insecurities
Sprout in many of ways.

The feeling
Of your worthiness
Burned to ashes
And the feeling
Of wholesomeness
Is pieced away.

Loneliness
Is the reminder
Of love.
Where insecurities
Are to be altered
As service to self.

Where ashes spread
And blossom many qualities
To the surface.
And the feeling
Of connection
Serves in all places.

It's up to you,
To make an adventure in life.

Pull away
The curtains
Of self-judgement
And seek
The strength
Of your love.

The next moment
Will not be the same as the current
As it will become the last.

We should be more like a jellyfish,
Flowing graciously through the mysterious motion
of nature
And to follow the motion of our emotions to sway us
in navigation.

The more blood circulation.
The more love circulation.

Through the release
Of life's rubbish,
Arises a new
And refined
Intention.

Be ignited
By all of
Life's wonders.

Unfold feelings that were puzzling
Into a vision of clarity.

Your journey
Showcases the ability
To survive
Time and time again.

To feel secure
In the embodiment
Of who you are,
Sprouts from the love
That you nourish
Yourself with.

Turn the feeling
Of delicately placing
Your footsteps
On sinking sand,

Into a moment
Of sharpening
Your weapon
Of strength.

No matter
The highs and lows
Of life's roller coaster,
The sky
Is always visible.

The beginning of any journey
Is always a rough path,
But you are there
To construct and pave it
Along the way.

Journey
Through
The night

To catch
The rising of
The light.

Lead the way,
My Heart.

The moment
Are the seeds
To what will
Flourish in the future.

No matter
The lack
Of pillars
You have,

You still
Can uncover
A way to be
Poised in life.

Our faces have a structural landscape.
Formed by hilly and smooth surfaces,
Rigid and bowed lines,
Various hues and expressions.
Similar to the landscapes you often
Set your eyes in awe to.

Enduring

I am here
In the moment
Of feeling.

I am here
In the moment
Of being.

Being here
Is the moment
That impacts
The moments
Ahead for me.

Listen within
From within
You are beyond.

Feel the bitterness of the dark
To ignite the warmth inside.

Dream

Of the good things,

Aim

For the dreams,

Live

The good things.

Power,
In my definition,
Is the ability to move
With a kindred force
Catapulted by the dark experiences
That gifted you with lessons
And to own that power.
To embrace the dark
That which you overcame
And using that power furthermore
To inspire.

In order
To get the
Big picture.

In order
To smell the
Open blossom
Of a flower.

Begins
At the planting
Of a little seed.
And another.
And another.

Moving on can be a heavy force
When the moments you cherish the most
Comes to be a memory.
But you find yourself hoping
Those moments to prolong
For the reason that your heart
Tangles around it tightly.

Yet, life propels,
Stretching that cord
As you feel yourself
Resisting it from tearing.
But as a result
It tears anyways
While snapping back at your heart, hurting.

Otherwise, if you let it be
The cord wouldn't be cautioned
To tear and snap
Rather a cord doesn't exist at all
Because no matter what,
It belongs within your heart
Following your journey furthermore.

Your body
Is a wondrous vessel.
At times hallow
With nothing but the element
Of air remaining in it.
At times holding
The weight of water in it.

In a day
We are born
In the awakening
Of the light.

And we die
In the night.
And then it begins again
Time after time.

To be born
Into the conscious
And then leave
To the subconscious.

As what we plant
Through the day
Will root into the
Form of our being.

Still, we are redressed
To the deep scan of the darkness.
We intertwine ourselves
Through the dark to uncover
The deepest roots of that form.

And as the day awakens
We have the opportunity
To dig and to replant.
Altering the cycle
Of our units of time.

The only way to

Grow

Is to be

Rooted.

A flower opens
To the warm light
From above.
Sun bathing
Her in joy
Allowing her
To free her petals
From tucking
Into the centre.

Her roots deep
Into her mother,
Her ancestor,
And womanhood.
Absorbing her enriched
Emotional fluids
From deep within her.

Her aroma
Is of sweet innocence
And floral tender passion,
Captivating
The noses of many.

Her innate
Power of love.
Keeps her mighty
Unfolding
And flowering.

When the sun
No longer shines
Its warmth on her
And the bitter sensation
Reaches her,
She loses sense
Of her power
Closing and wilting
While her scent
Becomes bitter and offensive,
Steering the noses of others
Away from her presence.

Her droopy form
Curls her into hiding,
Her vibrancy alters
To dark and dimly,
Weakened and angry,
Losing touch
Of the flame
Left in her being.

Mother
Is calling to her,
To come inside
Her enriched fertility.
To hold her
To comfort her
To reconnect her
To the roots
Of which blossomed her
To the sun in the first place.

To be in the nourishment
Of her femininity
Her innate strength
Her emotions
And her undying vibrancy.

Within time,
As her mind
Takes seasons
Her ability to grow
And to be comforted
From the warmth above
Will be in activity.

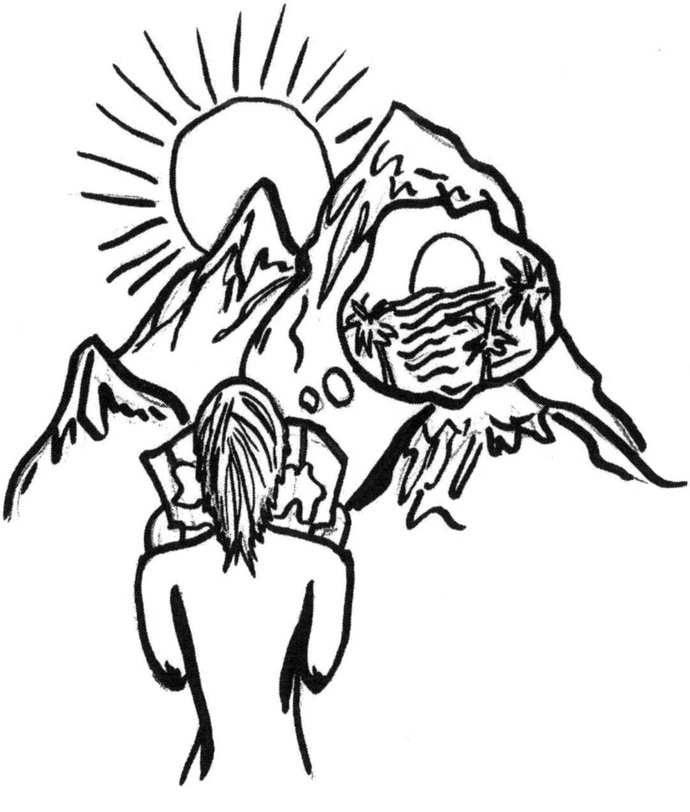

Eventually
You will grow
With sturdy roots
Able to reach you
To the height
You once
Foresaw.

Oftentimes
We search for love
A searching of validation
Of love through others
And searching for those
To love us.

We search
Beyond the frame
Of the love
That is already within us,
That we lose sight
Of the capture
Within completely.

It's not a matter of seeking,
It's a matter of feeling
That internal pulsation
Like a mallet rotating
Against the rim of a singing bowl
Birthing a striking vibration and sound
Unable to be ignored.

Feel the love,
Its deep emotions,
And the pulsation
That caresses your vessel
From within.

Dive through
The thick pool
Of water
To float
Atop

To be at ease
With your emotions,
You must dive
Deeply within it.

As you submerge yourself,
With an intake of just one
Breath of life force,
Into the afar
Of the darkest
Motion of water.

It hinges on
Your reaction
It hinges on
Your actions

That will trigger
How such a contact
Will provoke you
In either the fate
Of drowning in it
Or the fate
Of rising to the surface of it.

Your heart
Is magic

A magnet,
Hard to repel,

Its radiance
Difficult to shun.

Stop searching
Ahead
For answers.

Welcome your
Senses
To the answers.

The act
Of your parent
Brings you forward
In your journey.

Sometimes
You have to feel
The deepest pain
To set yourself
Free.

If the past
Seeps through
The cracks,
Allow it
Don't force
Its way back.

Earth
Is the womb
That holds the
Essence
Of warmth and vibration.

Her essence
Radiates in the form
Of many growth and intelligences.

A mother
A nurturer
A being of nourishment.

Her home offers
A sanctuary
Filled with nature of beauty
In diverse features and feelings

Earth
Is magical.
Beautiful
And sacred.

Show her love,
Help protect the home
That has been gifted to you.

Embrace Earth.

Stumps
Are for
Finding
Your
Footing.

There is a
Centre
To every branch
Parting.

Surrender,
Surrender to the moments
That feel ungrounded
That feel unsupported
That feel unstable.

Surrender,
Surrender to your heart
To deeply expand
And melt to earth.

Allow your heart
To be the reviving potion
That feeds your base
To grow and solidify.

The base of your life
The seed of your mind.

Surrender,
To allow your heart
To be the rich soil
That truly grows
And grounds you.

Surrender isn't being defeated
It's nothing to fear
It's absolute detachment.
Like stripping the heavy garments
Into your bare.

Its freedom,
The deepest relaxation
You can encounter.
It's defeating your demons
And the heavy cords with utter ease.

With surrender,
You become the most heroic being of peace.

Your life
Is your truth.
Truth is unalike
For all beings.

Your truth
Is moulded
By your story
Of the past
And all stories
Differ from one another.

Your truth
Is the result
From the graspings
Of the lessons,
Your digestion,
And what you seek ahead.

Focus on your truth
Don't veer to another's.
Yes, your truth will evolve
But propelled by your experience
And the absorption of knowledge
You take.

Focus on your truth.
As you remain seeded in your truth
Your heart ignites you on the embark ahead.

Don't dwell
Out of you
For answers.

Delve
Within you
At its deepest
For such answers
To be revealed.

Your life
Isn't linear.

Your life
Is made of
Terrains,
Hills,
Cliffs,
Endless bodies of water,
And the droughts of the desert.

We're made to explore them.
To experience the depths
Of our life's encounters,
To challenge our understanding,
And prevail with the lessons
That fuel our journey.

As you find adventure
With the outside of nature.
Find the adventure
With the internal nature.

How to see the clear sky
Beyond the clouds that shadow your vision
Of who you are,
Comes from your embarkation
To expand the grounds of where you go.

The more you stretch out
Your experiences,
The deeper
You discover yourself.

Through the journey
You'll be tested by your past,
Come to the awareness
Of the seeds that spoil you,
And lead you into the in-depth
Knowing of who you are.

You heal.
And as you heal from your aches and seeds,
You transform from them into stripping the layers,
To the discovery of your earthly core.

When you walk this world, do you ever feel the support beneath you,
Pulsating deeply through your soles,
Feeling your roots stand tall?

Feel the air caressing you, all around you?
Feel your heart as the ignition of all your motion?
Feel your breath roaming through your limbs
To make space for receiving and giving?

That is connection.
That is confidence,
Living through the life that was set up for you.

Live it.
Feel it.
Be it.
At all times.

Eyes
Are one
Sense

But a feeling
Is a sense
Of power.

Walked this long path
Drenched by the shedding
Of the heavy clouds.

Drops,
Tingling my body
Feeling touched deeply.

As the sky released
And I embraced that feeling
Then I too felt the release within.

When the sky
Shed its tears
The sunshine
Then appeared.

Brighter and warmer
Reflecting the light
Within my heart.

Day-to-day
As you nourish
Your plants
So in time
They will
Grow.

When you change
Your view
Of the icky glue
That sticks onto you,
The substance then weakens
And sheds off
Leaving you smooth and anew.

Often we fall
Into the habit
Of victimizing ourselves
As the centre
Of the negative world.
Such rubbish of mind's reasoning
Doesn't improve you
Nor your environment.

For why would anyone
Want to be fueled by rubbish?

Devotion
Is the energy
Of change
And creation.

The act
Of committing
Is an adoration
Of where you
Feel deeply
Your journey
Should be.

This has been an icky time
I say for most of us.
We may have been too much mind risen,
Swamped, and thinly pointed.
We may have felt
Out of our element,
Concealed by the fog.
But look around,
You aren't solo on such a journey.

Look at the weather
And how it insightfully reenacts
Our inner journey.

She is bracing to the motion
Through an alter to the warmer states ahead
Yet doses of her past, the gloomy states,
Are preserving.
Leaving the conditions
Of her landscape dressed in sheer ice and syncing mud.

Strolling through such an unsteady path
While wholly seeking the horizon,
Certainly strikes us in a daze,
Slipping on the surface of the past,
Feeling stuck and engulfed
In the icky mind.

But it's your ongoing grit
To visit such terrains with grace,
To motion at a slow pace,
And to stretch through it,
Perhaps other routes
Till your stride pauses
To a point of end.

Being in the moment
Is being with divine.

Consciousness is the sound
Between the instrument and the player.
The consciousness
Is a moment in presence
Beyond the measure of time.

With your heart
Devoted to that moment,
You serve divine.
Planting yourself
As that sound
Between the instrument and the action.

Life flows in and out of our lungs.
It awakens every parcel of who we are.
Offering us the energy to sling towards our aims.
To make the days ahead better than the days of the past.

Life gathers the reminder of then,
The making of the moment,
And hopes of what is ahead.
They join together in a pool of unity
Streaming through our beings.

Life,
For our children,
And our children's children.

For those we love,
Our neighbors,
And the beings that surround us in this moment.

For our ancestors,
The lineage that navigated us to where we anchor in this moment,
Honouring them as we pass on the values from one age to another.

As we breathe now,
Feel the power that roars through your lungs.

Even if the clouds
Cover the sky,
The sun is always
Beaming behind it.

Life flows like a river,
Therefore, it alters.
There is a coming and a going.
A receiving and a giving.
And a nourishing and a releasing.

Look at your life as an opportunity
each time you awake,
Sailing on that mindset throughout your day
As you allow the waves to move you,
Riding over one to another.

Our past is a pillar
To how we ground ourselves
In our lifting form.

The form of you
That perches above one step to another
Leading your heart to grow.

Between what holds us
And what lifts us
Is our emotional weight.

If we hold emotionally too heavily,
It bears a burden on the very pillars
That stands us firmly.

To lug less force
Against the columns
That holds us up,
Occurs by the opening portal
Of our emotions
To release like water spilling out.

We can't force ourselves onto the surface,
If we have no deep ground to push from.
Plunge down into the ground to receive.
Receiving the knowledge from deep within.
To explore, to observe, and to accept.

As you sprout from that surrounding,
It offers you the lifting energy.
Enough to the assertive warmth
That pulls you from the ground
And into the centre of it all.

Time ages quickly,
Yet we spend those short fragments of time
Serving to the expectations in our life.
And in a mere conscious moment…
We notice we are older.
Our parents and loved ones too around us.

Swimming in the waves of regret.
Scoping in the past to rewrite
Some memories to the category of what ifs.
Not able to have desired experiences
Swirling in us with the reward of bliss.

Because time ages quickly,
That when we leave our desires to the last,
We will be too wrinkled and near to death,
Draped by the heavy debts.
Still serving to the expectations
Of what we served in the past.

Within, we are depressed
That we didn't live our days
To the fullest as we wished we had.
Acting in the world by our bitter jealousy,
Suppressing the young ones too from living their dreams.

Because we are influenced
By the wave like a domino onto the next.
Repressing the inner growth
From one wave to the other,
That collides and stunts
The water from rising and falling
By its own time individually

Time ages quickly,
That those short fragments of time
Should be a conscious collection
Of moments we thrived.
Where we struggled on the path
We innately wanted to take
And grew our weapon of strength.
Where we expanded our views
Of the landscapes outwardly and inside our beings.
Where we followed the way
Our heart pulled us to take.
Where we tried and where we made it life.

Because time ages quickly
That we are here, in this life,
To make those fragments last
By much meaning and quality
To hold infinitely through our journey.

So make your life,
And its tiny fragments of time
Worth to live as fully as you can.
Because one day
We'll notice that we are a decade older
And another, and another.
Wasting the time we have.

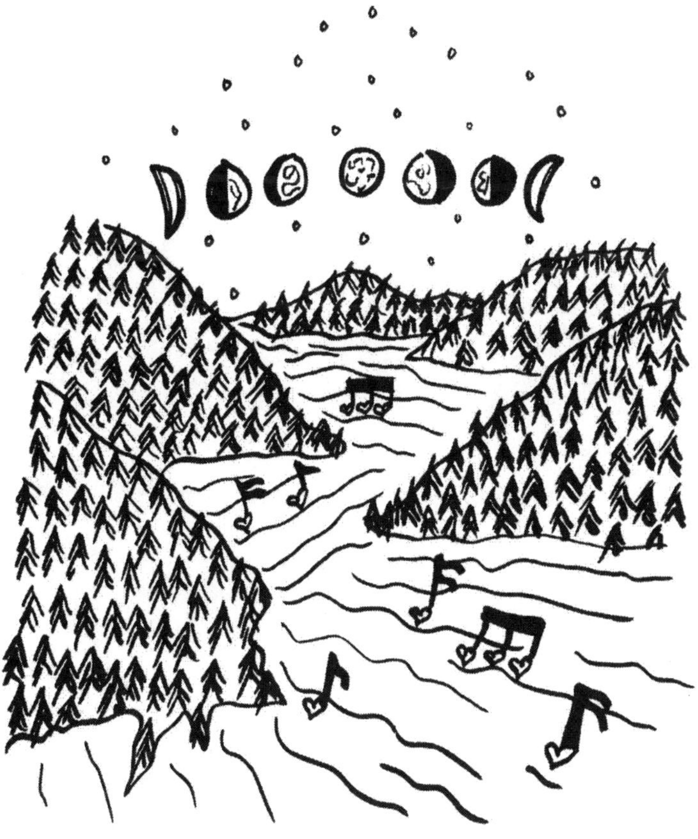

The more you doubt yourself,
The less you become yourself.

The crossroads we face
Not only brings us to the centre of the crossroads,
But to the centre of ourselves.

Stand firmly on where your roots dig deeply in.
Have the weight of your aim sync them deeper.
No matter how small you may seem to feel.
No matter how fearful it may seem to be.
Because what surrounds you, was made for you.
Was made for you to stand firmly with.

Don't feel you are on a lonely road
When there are many of roads.

When we express verbally,
It's like making wind through the trees
That blows off the leaves.

To flee from our stumps
Are much easier than to overcome them.
But fleeing leaves no footing for outcome
As much as the mastery gained
When you challenge yourself.

Challenge is facing within
Your confusion and discomfort.
To scope your internal and outer worlds
With a lens of great size for the aim
Of observation and reflection.

Mastery is your will
To summon the inner fighters,
Born into their role of bringing fear,
To rise onto the surface
And to combat those aggressors.

Disconnection syncs you deeply
Into the realm of the unknown,
To offer you time to sit with it
Without your resistance.

Notice what you find there and observe it.

The more expanded we become
On the surface of the path we take,
The more roadblocks we will face.
The more welcoming we will be.
For just as evenly, we will face
The many detours to freely take.

From one season to the next.
From one self-alter onto the next.
Becomes ever changing of the features our life takes.
To make life as a vast and expanded space.

Choices are the directions
Of where the flow appears and moves to.

The fluctuations
Like a stirring wave we sail on,
Is the teacher
In finding the balance
To which we face.

In order to know what is good for us,
We must face the parts
That seem uninviting to us.

You never truly fall.
You never are a face of the unloved.
You never are the mistakes that have come.
You are in the process of finding.
And only when we lose some footing
Can we acknowledge how we can strengthen
The ability to stand on our feet firmly.

When it flows, it flows.
When it doesn't…
Well, you can't make the river flow in your direction.

Life fades away
Or so it seems
It leaves me in the bare floating endlessly.
My skin glimmering by the sparkles of stars
That caress me without touching.

Wholesome, I am.
Wholesome is my haven
From which I can deeply breathe.

An awakening,
One upon the other,
Unfolding a petal and a petal
Till the flower opens.

Tender heat
So holy and devotional,
Not one for the wicked
Nor the sinful.

But what we invoke
Behind the power of the flame,
Will summon either
The brightened or darkened
Entries to claim.

Mating,
A heavenly gathering to ignite the flame,
Though we are already a part of the fire
That roams within the vessels we take,
Deeply connected to all things
Created in its name.

This heat I feel when I breathe,
I feel when the water caresses me,
And all subtleties that come into contact of me.

Between two beings,
It is a beautiful matching to strike a flame,
Though claiming our own fire within
Burns down the cages
Into an opening space
Of freedom to explore with a mate.
My inner fire
Is a sacred altar
That only welcomes
Those that have the calmness

To wait and to hold space
Until granted to join me.

Therefore, a frontier
Is laid to protect the holy altar
From any attackers or stealers
Of the sacred fire that is within me.

GROWING

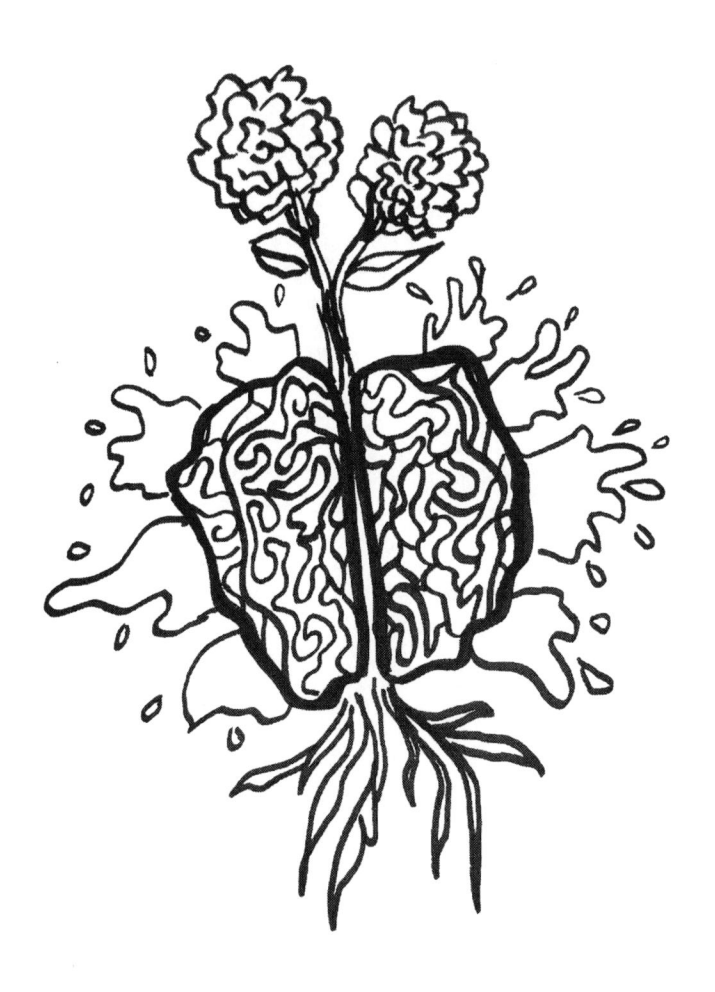

You see how vast the world is?
It was created for you.
It's here for you to explore and navigate through.
For your vision to be vast and opened,
Not narrowed and blinded.

You see how layered your body is?
It was created for you.
It's here for you to explore and navigate through.
For your feelings to be vast and opened,
Not weighted and hidden.

You see how complex your mind is?
It was created for you.
It's here for you to explore and navigate through.
For your thoughts and emotions
To be coherent and opened
Not patterned and negative.

How will you choose to use what is created for you?

To the day,
As everything
Becomes a moment.

Your storms
Will come to be
Beautiful days.

Seasons don't reverse,
They change forward.

Life is about
Moving through doors
Not standing
In the frames of them.

You are never truly deserted to the land of the lone.
You are never tussling solo
for we all have a road of barricades and detours.
You may seem alone on the road you take,
But there are many of roads,
Many others alongside yours
Who are taking their rough road on the way ahead.
We are deeply connected, beside one another,
on the paths we take.

Rebirth of the seasons is at a near.
The touch of the weather is becoming milder
as the days go by.
We are awakening more and more.
Unfolding one petal to the next.
As we open, our heart welcomes so much in.
The light will be seen more through the days
And opportunities will indeed reach to us
more than we think.
Unfold the petals of your heart,
Awaken more and more.

Peel me apart.
All the flaking skin
That sticks on.

The many layers
That cover me
And cover me.

Masking the true me
That dwells within me.
That dwells, waiting.

Waiting for the moment to be free.
Free from what I've been told I am.
Free from what I've been told to believe.
Free from disconnecting, from me.

The true me is within me.

Never forget your inner youth.
May everyday be anew.

Follow your deepest calling.
No matter how muted the sound may seem
Because it's there and it can be heard,
Just listen and as you listen allow the sound to grow.

From the bitter and wilted,
Comes gentle sprouting of good news.
Comes beauty to shine in the eyes of bypassers
And for them to shine too.
Beauty can grow from this
And beauty will be a new route to walk through.
Always, will something sprout.

I find my footsteps
Slowly and pleasantly
Caressing up one and the other,
Leading me to gracefully
Rise with glee
Like a gentle swan
Spreading its striking wings.

I've been listening
To the soft calls.
These calls motioning me
To one destination and the next,
To awaken the big calls ahead.
The type of calls
That allow my striking wings to spread.

And who knows where these steps will locate me next.
I just have a feeling that they will be bigger calls
Too shakingly loud to mute away.

Mind is like a reflector to what one sees.

Feeling into this human form.
Swept by sadness, fear, death, anger, and frustration
Like rapid winds hitting against the body,

Much like a hurricane bringing mess into what was once home.

In the journey of rediscovering home—the heart.
Having to gather the broken pieces as food for the fire.
To have it bring warmth within and bring about
new beginnings.

Sometimes we have to search
But sometimes we need to pause and see what searches for us.

There is no language that can define what life is.
Life is a feeling.

Amongst the debris,
There roams beautiful creatures.

Growth…
It will always appear.

Strive to the places
That not only surround you,
But nourish you.

Swifting life's struggles away
To bring my bare emotions forward
To be seen.

As streams run thick,
Clashes of water consist,
The clap-like waves of static
Pulsing the skins of our bodies.
As if time ran longer
Bringing us to the sounds of the moment,
And having our senses vibrate even faster.

Be on the edge of the surface,
To see life outside the borders.
And know that there are
Greater heights to roam,
There are bigger surfaces to know.

One wee drop,
One wee fall of impact,
Lets ripples and motion
Move from the centre out
And out till the whole of the surface
Feels the movement.

Unearthing the grounds below,
To rippling it as it awakens us
To what the nature of our soul is—
To the nature of what life is.

Sometimes we walk a step forward,
Sometimes we leap our way ahead,
And sometimes we dive into the depths
Of our internal motions
To cleanse the path
Where our sights land.

There.
Right there.
Is a creation that is deeply touching.
A creation so surreal that your mind doesn't want to acknowledge it.

And here it is,
All to ourselves.
Where only us amongst its waters.
Where only the sound of our voices,
The ducks, and our paddles tapping the water—
Echoing through one valley to another.

No other human but us.
Only ripples of our movement
Touching the motion of the still waters.
Viewing the depths and layers
Of the endless mountains.

There.
Right there.
Is a creation that was made for us in that moment.

Curiously seeking
What shows up for me
Like scoping the vast sky
To find life moving above me.

The sky cries
As the anger roars
And the truth strikes
Through the sheaths of us.

But through this comes release
Through this comes a clearness
Through this comes a bridge
To the many forms of us.

Fall is upon,
Upon to unveil the layers.
One upon the other,
That drapes onto us.
To soon bring us into our bare—
To feel rebirthed.

Water is around me now.
Endless, it is.
Not knowing how deep it becomes
Nor how shallow it is.
The tides, arriving and leaving.
The waves, gliding and crashing.
We will only truly know
Once it calls us to go in.

LET LIFE BE BRIGHT

In Loving Memory

Of those near that passed on during
the flow of these insights

To my grandmother,

Virginia Kearse

To my furry baby,

Jill

To my grandfather,

Eduardo Benevides

To my furry buddy,

Ruckus

With Gratitude

These moments, even the moments we tend to ignore for the pain they erupt in us, are the flickers that have grown me. As I grow, I find myself constructing my dreams into reality. As for the moments of complete lightness, they allowed me to feel the orgasmic sensations that God brings to us. For that, I am immensely grateful for being here experiencing all that I can and moulding my perception of life. I am thankful for life/God/Universe, the events, and the beings that have occurred. I feel more clarity to it all yet I have much more to discover.

I am beyond grateful for those who encouraged me to express my creativity and understanding of these moments, to those who felt moved by my expressions and writings. To those that allow me to guide them into their own personal practice and discoveries. Without them, this book wouldn't have become animated; wouldn't have been born.

I am sincerely filled with gratitude for my family and friends who support my growth and endeavours in an ongoing direction, although the transitions into my reality maybe weren't always understood or seen with the clearest of eyes in the beginning. I am forever hoping as they allow me to see my light, that they witness theirs.

I am deeply thankful for the guidance of The Awakened Press, for Lindsay R. Allison to have held my hand while constructing this to be seen by the masses. For making the process a bit more at ease as I made my personal findings into a finding for others to see.

And I thank you, for taking the time to delve into the expressions that have flowed to me, to witness my growth and comprehension, my response and results, and to explore your own transformations.

My deepest gratitude,

Felecia

Felecia Kearse, Yoga Teacher and Meditation Guide, was trained for a year under a Hindu and Vedic Priest in Ontario, Canada between 2016-2017. Since then ripples of awareness were felt against her, scoping life into a striking view that formed into these writings.

Felecia has been blessedly sighted for a nomination for Best Yoga Instructor in the Orangeville Readers' Choice Awards 2019. She was completely transformed by yoga, having healed herself from lifelong issues. She unravelled new depths of herself that induced levels of awareness to reflect on her past and come to the answers of why life brought her to where she is. This encouraged her to see life differently and as she did, words began to flow through her in the form of writing. Countless times, friends and followers were either touched or inspired by her wordings. This brought her collection of poems and notes from her journal into a story.

Felecia is equally a lover of hiking as she is with her yoga practice. She is a minimalist who lives in a relaxed small town surrounded by sandy beaches that she spends time in, taking her tries in surfing, and enjoying the mesmerizing views on the West Coast of British Columbia, Canada.

Felecia offers a range of yogic services on her platform Yoga Unearth Me, offering immersive yoga and meditation journeys between privates, workshops, an online course, event-based classes, and her podcast of the same name.

Find out more about her Yoga Guidance at:

www.yogaunearthme.com

Manufactured by Amazon.ca
Bolton, ON